SHAPES
ALIVE!

LEARNING RESOURCES®

OVERHEAD & MATH MANIPULATIVES

Enrich the activities in this book with the following manipulatives! See your local school supply dealer for more information on the complete line of Learning Resources' overhead and math products. For a dealer near you, call (800) 222-3909.

LER 120   **Geometric Solids**
Twelve hardwood 3-dimensional shapes including cones, sphere, cube, cylinders, pyramid, prisms, hemisphere and rectangular solids.

LER 152   **Rainbow Geoboards**
Colorful set of five 5 × 5 pin geoboards in 5 bright colors. Rubberbands included.

LER 152T   **Transparent Geoboard**
5 × 5 pin geoboard for use on the overhead projector. Rubberbands included.

LER 416   **Class-Pack Tangrams**
Includes 30 plastic tangram puzzles in 4 colors packaged in storage bucket.

LER 418   **Tangrams for the Overhead**
Four complete tangrams in bright transparent colors.

LER 286-6   **Rainbow Pentominoes**
Six pentomino sets scored in 1" segments in red, green, blue, yellow, purple, and orange. Storage tub included.

LER 415   **Overhead Pentominoes**
Scored, brightly-colored pentomino set for teacher demonstration.

LER 134   **Plastic Pattern Blocks**
Includes 250 blocks in 6 colors and 6 shapes, 2 plastic mirrors, and plastic storage tub.

LER 640   **Overhead Pattern Blocks**
49 transparent Pattern Blocks for whole-class teaching.

SHAPES ALIVE!

Exploring shapes
for grades 3–6

Neville Leeson

Published with the permission of Dellasta Pty. Ltd.

© revised 1993 Learning Resources, Inc., Lincolnshire, Illinois 60069.

First published 1990 by Dellasta Pty. Ltd., Mount Waverley, Victoria, Australia.

ISBN 1-56911-000-X (previously ISBN 0-947138-56-0)

Printed in the United States of America.

Contents

**Challenging Extension
   Activities:**

CURVED OR STRAIGHT

1 Find five different curved lines in the classroom.

2 Find five different straight lines in the classroom.

3 Mark two points on a piece of paper like this:

•

•

Join these two points with a straight line. Then join them with a curved line.

4 Are the following curved or straight:
a rivers
b flagpoles
c train lines
d electric power lines
e edges of a doorway?
Can you give reasons why each of these is curved and/or straight?

A VARIETY OF SHAPES

1 Make a variety of shapes (three-sided, four-sided, . . .) using:
  a rope or string
  b pop-sticks.

2 Use a geoboard and rubber bands to make a variety of triangles. How do they differ? In what ways are they similar?

3 Use a geoboard to make a variety of four-sided figures. Can you name some of them?

4 Choose a solid shape and hold it under a strong light so that it forms a shadow. What shape is the shadow?

5 Which solids will form shadows of the following shapes:
  a triangle
  b square
  c circle
  d rectangle?

SHAPE WALK

Walk around the outside of your school building and make a chart of all the shapes used to build it.

Shape	Where used

SYMMETRICAL FIGURES

Use a mirror to complete the following symmetrical figures:

LINES OF SYMMETRY

In each of the following pictures draw in the line of symmetry:

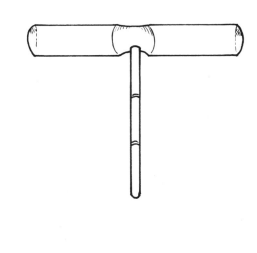

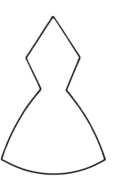

PAINT-BLOB SYMMETRY

Let us make a symmetrical design.

1 Fold a rectangular piece of paper in half:

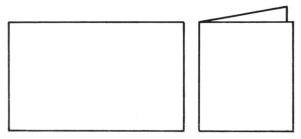

2 Open it out and put some blobs of paint on one half:

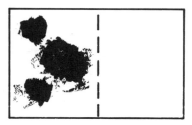

3 Close it up and press down on it.

4 Open it out and notice the symmetry.

PAPER CUTTING AND SYMMETRY

Take a square piece of paper, fold it in half, then fold it in half again. Cut small pieces out of this (while it is folded). Now open it out and note the symmetry that you have formed.

SYMMETRY OF LETTERS OF THE ALPHABET

1 Mark in lines of symmetry for each letter of the alphabet. (You may use a mirror to help you.)

A   B   C   D   E   F

G   H   I   J   K   L

M   N   O   P   Q   R

S   T   U   V   W   X

Y   Z

2 Which letters have exactly one line of symmetry?

3 Which letters have more than one line of symmetry?

4 Invent your own symbol so that it has one line of symmetry.

COMPLETING SYMMETRY

1 Complete these shapes in the same way as the first one so that the dotted line is an axis of symmetry:

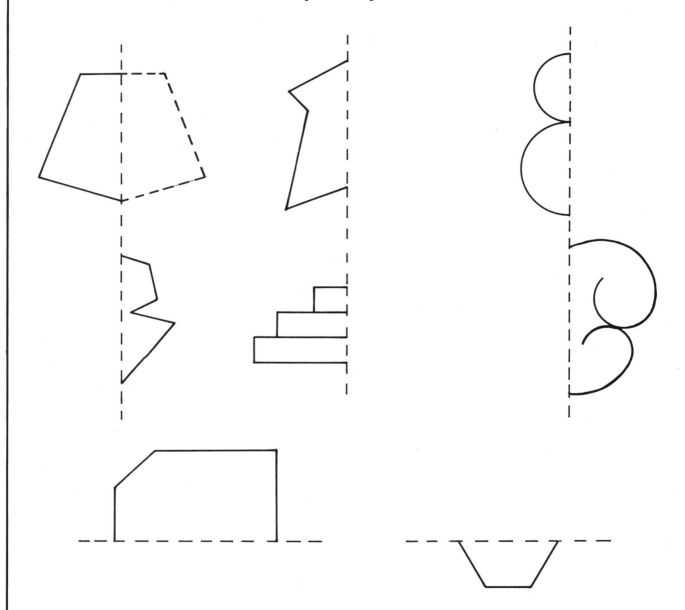

2 On a piece of paper draw some half-shapes as above and then ask your neighbor to complete them so that they are symmetrical.

WALLPAPER SYMMETRY

Obtain some pieces of wallpaper and carefully examine the patterns. Can you find examples of symmetry?

SYMMETRICAL SHAPES ON DOT PAPER

Draw shapes on dot paper and draw in lines of symmetry (where they occur); for example, can you find an axis of symmetry for this shape?

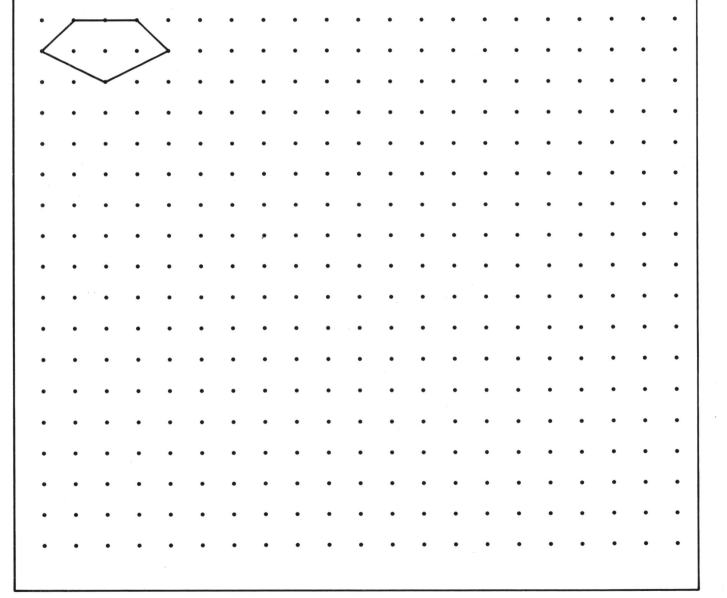

TESSELLATING WITH SHAPES

1 **a** Obtain some square tiles all the same size as this one:

b Use them to cover this rectangle:

c Do they tessellate (i.e. fit together without gaps or overlaps)?

2 **a** Obtain some circular tiles (all the same size).
b Place them on your table so that they touch each other.
c Do they tessellate?

3 **a** Obtain a set of equilateral triangles (all the same size).
b Use them to make a larger equilateral triangle.
c Do they tessellate?

4 **a** Can you find some other shapes that tessellate?
b Can you find some other shapes that do not tessellate?

A FIVE-PIECE TANGRAM

1 Make a five-piece tangram as follows:

a Fold a square piece of paper in half and cut along the fold line:

b Cut along the diagonal of one of these pieces:

c Fold and cut the other piece into two smaller squares:

d Fold and cut one of these smaller squares in half:

e You should have five pieces:

2 Reform the square from these five pieces.

3 Make other shapes using all five pieces.

MAKING THE SEVEN-PIECE TANGRAM

Make a seven-piece tangram as follows:

1   Obtain a square piece of paper of side 10 cm.

2   Join a pair of opposite corners (B and D in the figure below).

3   By measuring (or by folding) find the midpoints E and F of AB and AD respectively.

4   Join E and F.

5   By placing your ruler edge on A and C, draw a portion of the diagonal from A to C. Name the points G and H as shown in the figure.

6   Obtain J (the midpoint of BH). Join E and J.

7   Obtain K (the midpoint of DH). Join G and K.

8   Cut out the seven shapes.

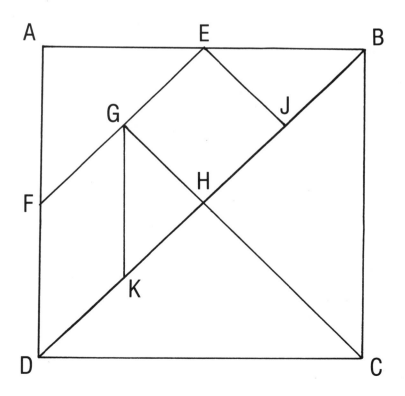

EXPLORING WITH TANGRAMS

Use a seven-piece tangram set for the following explorations:

1 Can you form a triangle using exactly three tangram pieces? Here is one possible solution:

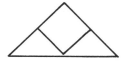

but there are other possibilities. See how many you can find.

2 Cover this shape using:
  a two pieces
  b four pieces
  c five pieces.

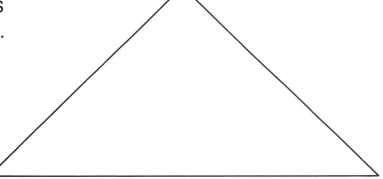

3 Can you form a triangle using all seven pieces?

4 Can you form squares from two, three, four, five, or seven pieces?

5 Can you also form parallelograms using two or more pieces?

6 How can you show that these three shapes have the same area?

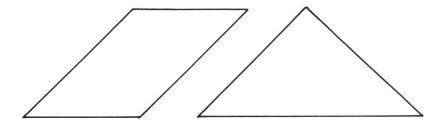

COVERING SHAPES WITH TANGRAMS

Use a set of tangram pieces to cover these shapes:

MAKING SHAPES WITH TANGRAMS

1 Use a set of tangram pieces to make figures similar to these:

2 Use a set of tangram pieces to make your own shape.

RIGID SHAPES

1. Make a triangle from three different geostrip pieces. (If geostrips are unavailable, you could use thin strips of cardboard of varying lengths. Each strip could have a hole punched near each end. Strips can be joined using paper fasteners.)

2. Make some four-sided shapes from geostrips, for example a rectangle, square. Compare them with the triangle. Can any be pushed out of shape? If so what can be done to prevent this?

3. Use geostrips to make a pentagon (five-sided shape). Can it be pushed out of shape? How many diagonal strips will make it rigid?

4. Can you explain why triangles are used in building construction?

5. Find pictures or make drawings of where triangles are used in building construction.

FORMING TRIANGLES

1. Obtain four straws and three pieces of pipe cleaner.

2. Cut the straws to lengths of 4 cm, 5 cm, 7 cm, 10 cm.

3. Guess how many different triangles you could make from these straws.

4. Check your estimate by making as many as you can.

5. If you had an extra straw 15 cm long, how many extra triangles could you now make?

FINDING AND DRAWING CIRCLES

1 Find examples of man-made circles (circular faces of objects) in real life.

2 Find examples of circles in nature.

3 In how many ways can you draw a circle?
Try these:
  a Draw a circle using a compass.
  b Draw a circle using a pencil, a piece of string, and a thumb tack.
  c Obtain a circle by tracing around a cylinder.
  d Can you obtain a circle by using your span (tip of thumb to tip of little finger of outstretched hand)?
  e Can you think of other ways of forming circles?

4 Find out what concentric circles are. Draw some.

CUTTING BOXES AND PACKETS

1 Find a cardboard box (such as a chalk box) without a top. Cut along some of its edges so that you can open it out to form a *net* like this:

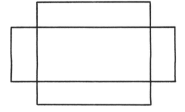

2 **a** Find other boxes or packets with tops.
  b Cut along some of their edges so that you can open them out to form their nets.
  c Draw their nets. ·

WHAT CAN YOU SEE?

1   **a**   Place a chalk box on the table.
     b   Look at one of its side faces.
     c   What shape can you see?
     d   Can you see any parallel lines? Which ones?
     e   What angles can you see?

2   Turn the box slightly and describe what you can see now.

3   Look down on the box from above and describe what you can see.

4   Stand a cylinder on one end and describe what you can see when looking at it from:
     a   the side
     b   above.

5   Match up the objects with their top and side views, using dotted lines (as partly shown):

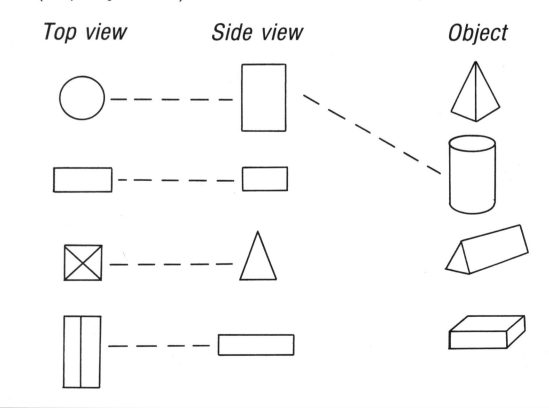

Top view   *Side view*   *Object*

MAKING AND EXAMINING PRISMS

1 Make these solid shapes:
- a rectangular prism.
- a square prism.
- a cube.

(You may use the nets supplied
and/or pipe cleaners and straws.)

2 Compare these solid shapes. In what way
are they similar? How do they differ?
Which one has all of its faces the same?

3 Find at least three examples of each,
either inside or outside the classroom.

4 What shape can you form from a pile of
square slices of bread (or from square
tiles)?

TRIANGULAR PRISMS

1 What shape can you make from a pile of triangular tiles?

2 Copy this net onto light cardboard and make a triangular prism:

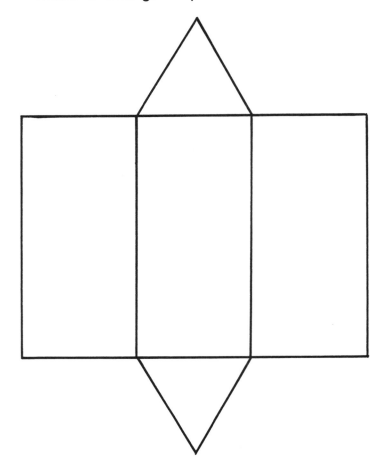

3 How many faces has it? What shapes are the faces?

4 Also make a triangular prism from straws and pipe cleaners.

5 Find at least three examples of triangular prisms.

INVESTIGATING SQUARE PYRAMIDS

1   Make a square pyramid using the net below or from pipe cleaners and straws:

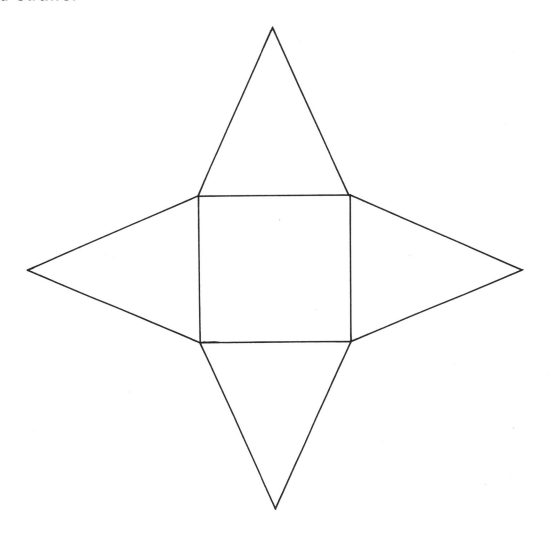

2   How many faces has it? What shapes are the faces?

3   Find information about the pyramids of Egypt.

4   Find other examples of pyramids.

Extension: Use two square pyramids and a square prism to make a Chinese lantern.

STRAIGHTNESS

1 Find examples of straight lines:
a inside the classroom
b outside the classroom.

2 With the help of a partner, pull tight a piece of string. Does it form a straight line? Sight along it.

3 How can a gardener plant straight rows of seedlings? (Use the same procedure in your garden.)

4 How are straight lines obtained for:
a lanes in swimming races
b lanes for athletic events
c boundaries for sporting fields?

5 Is the edge of your ruler straight?
a Place it on a sheet of paper and draw a pencil line along it.
b Turn the page upside down but not the ruler. Now see how the line fits the edge of the ruler.

6 Use your straightedge to test the flatness of a surface. If a surface is flat, there will be an even streak of light between it and the straight edge of the ruler. Test your desk top for flatness. Also test a cupboard door.

FOLLOWING DIRECTIONS

1   **a** Mark a point on the playground.

    b Walk 8 paces north, then 3 paces east, then 5 paces south, then 7 paces west, then 6 paces south, then 4 paces east, and then 3 paces north.

    c Where did you finish?

2   Make up a similar walk for a classmate.

3   Now follow these directions:

- Select a starting point; go 2 paces forward, turn right; go 4 paces forward, turn right; go 2 paces forward, turn right; go 4 paces forward, turn right.

Where did you finish?

4   Can you predict where this walk will finish before you walk it?

- Select a starting point; go 3 paces forward, turn right, 2 paces forward, turn left, 2 paces forward, turn left, 2 paces forward, turn right, 4 paces backwards.

5   Give directions for this:

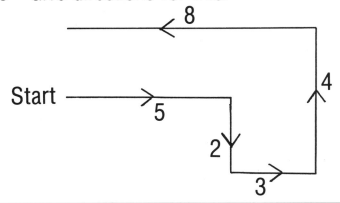

SYMMETRY FROM SHADING SQUARES

Complete shapes by shading squares to make a pattern that balances about lines of symmetry (shown by dotted lines); for example, complete the shading shown below so that there is symmetry.

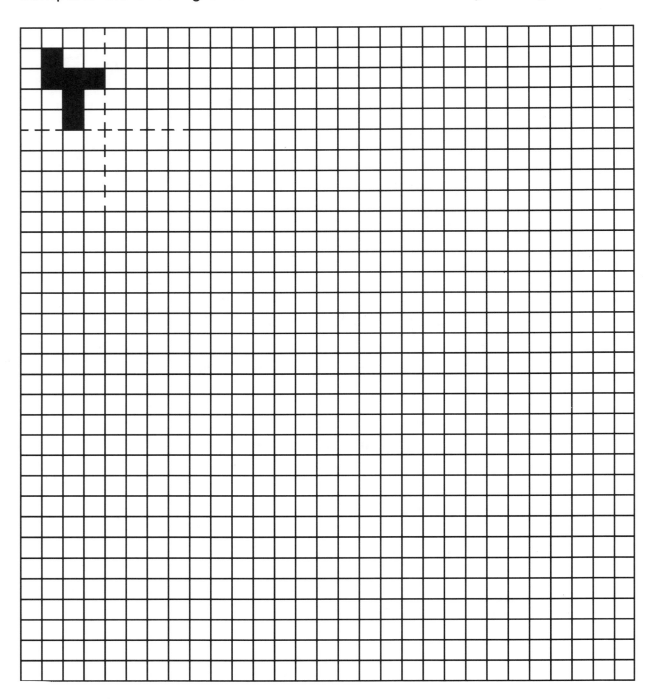

FINDING AXES OF SYMMETRY

1 How many axes of symmetry has a *square*? Select a square piece of paper and find how many different ways you can fold it in half (so that the two parts overlap exactly).

2 Repeat for a *rectangle*. Are the diagonals axes of symmetry?

3 Take a *circular* piece of paper. Fold it in half, open it out and fold in half using a different fold line, and so on. How many axes of symmetry has a circle?

SHAPES FROM SQUARES

1 Copy these two *squares* onto a piece of paper and cut out each one:

2 Can you make a symmetrical shape by placing these two squares so that they have at least one point or one line in common (i.e. so that they touch at a point or in a line)?

3 How many different shapes can you form in this manner?

CYLINDERS, CONES, AND SPHERES

1 Sort a class set of solids into those with:
   a at least one curved surface
   b no curved surfaces.

2 Sort the first group (with curved surfaces) into:
   a cylinders
   b cones
   c spheres
   d other shapes.

3 In what way are the shapes just sorted:
   a similar
   b different?

4 Find examples outside the classroom of:
   a cylinders
   b cones
   c spheres.

5 Can you find a cylinder joined to another solid shape?

6 Find pictures of cylinders, cones, and spheres.

CYLINDERS

1 How many different kinds of cylinders can you find in your classroom?

2 How many can you find outside?

3 Why are they so useful?

4 Can you think of a disadvantage of such shapes?

5 Make a construction using cylinders (e.g. a robot, an animal).

INVESTIGATING CYLINDERS

1 Find a soup can. What shape is it? Take off its label and open it out. What shape is it?

2 Fold a rectangular sheet of paper to form a cylinder.

3 By making a pile of coins, form a cylinder.

4 Copy this net onto a piece of light cardboard and make a cylinder:

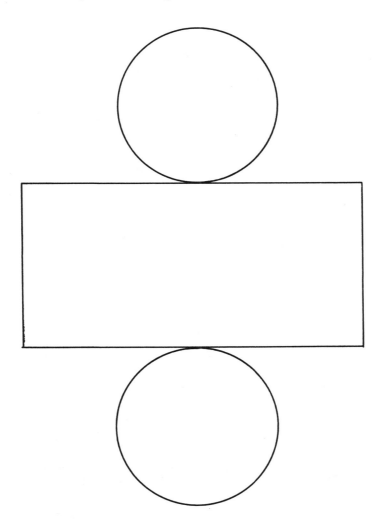

5 Why do you think bottles are cylindrical?

CIRCULAR DESIGNS

1 Draw a circle and then with the same radius show that it can be marked off six times around the circle.

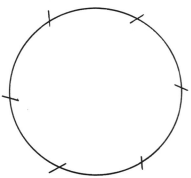

2 Using the same radius throughout, form this design:

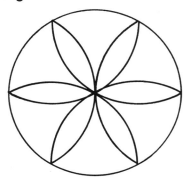

3 Now try this design and shade it as shown:

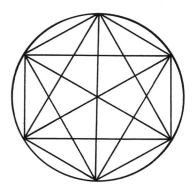 

4 Make a design of your own and shade it.

INVESTIGATING CIRCLES

1 Trace a circle onto a piece of paper and then cut out the circular shape. Fold it in half.

2 This fold line is called the diameter; it is an axis of symmetry. How many axes of symmetry does a circle have?

3 Each half of a circle is called a semicircle. Does it have an axis of symmetry?

4 Find examples of semicircles within or outside the classroom.

5 Fold a circle in half and then in half again to obtain quarters. Each of these is called a quadrant. Has each quadrant an axis of symmetry?

6 Investigate the use of logs and wheels for transport. Use some small pieces of dowel rod to move a brick along your desk.

VERTICAL AND HORIZONTAL LINES

1 a Make a plumb-bob (using a piece of string with a weight attached to one end).
b Use it to test for vertical lines in the classroom. Record four of them.
c Consider each example you chose. Would it matter if it wasn't vertical? Why or why not?

2 a Obtain a spirit level.
b Use it to find horizontal lines and surfaces. Record four of them.
c Would it make any difference if they were not horizontal?

3 a Find examples of perpendicular lines (lines at right angles to each other). Record two of them.
b If two lines are perpendicular, does one have to be horizontal and the other vertical?

SPECIAL TRIANGLES

1 Using a geoboard make as many different kinds of triangles as you can. In what way do they differ from one another?

2 Did you make any triangles with exactly two sides equal? These are called isosceles triangles. (The word "isosceles" comes from two Greek words meaning "equal legs".)

3 Perhaps you also made these:
- An equilateral triangle (having all three sides equal).
- A scalene triangle (with all sides unequal in length).
- A right-angled triangle (with one angle a right angle).

Isosceles triangle   Equilateral triangle   Scalene triangle   Right-angled triangle

4 Can you make (or draw) a right-angled isosceles triangle?
Is it possible to make a right-angled equilateral triangle?

5 Examine a set of swings and note the triangles that occur. Why are such shapes used?

6 If you can, observe corner posts of farm fences. How are they supported? Draw a diagram and comment on the triangles that occur.

7 How are triangles used in designing shelves attached to walls?

8 List at least six other occurrences of different types of triangles (isosceles, equilateral, right-angled) in the environment and describe why you think they have been used.

9 Draw an isosceles triangle on a piece of paper. Cut it out. By folding it, show that it has only one axis of symmetry. Can you find any equal angles?

10 Using a cutout of an equilateral triangle, find how many axes of symmetry it has. Also check for any equal angles.

INVESTIGATING PARALLEL LINES

1 Place a ruler on your page and draw a straight line along each edge of it: What are these lines called?

2 Can you find examples of parallel lines? Record three of them.

3 Measure the distance between a pair of parallel lines at various points along them. (For example, measure the distance between two wires of a fence at various places.) What did you find?

4 Why should these be parallel:
   a railway lines
   b fence wires
   c edges of a door?

5 Make a design using parallel lines.

6 Obtain two straight sticks (e.g. chop sticks) and lay them on the table so that a marble may roll along them. How did you place the sticks?

CURVES FROM STRAIGHT LINES

1 Draw an angle and mark off eight equally spaced points along each arm. Number them as shown. Then draw intervals to join corresponding numbers:

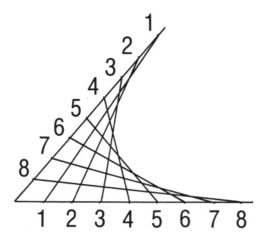

2 Complete this design:

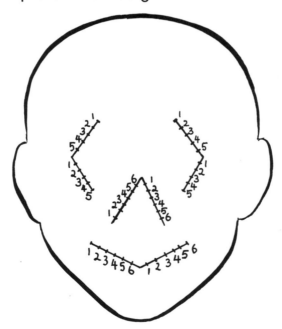

3 Try a design of your own.

FORMING ANGLES

1 What are:

   a acute angles

   b obtuse angles

   c right angles

   d straight angles?

2 Using a model clock face, move the hands to form each of the angles listed above.

3 Form each of the angles using geostrips.

4 Find examples of each in the classroom.

AN ANGLE TESTER

1 Take a piece of paper and fold it roughly in half.

2 Now fold the folded edge back along itself thus producing a right angle at the double fold.

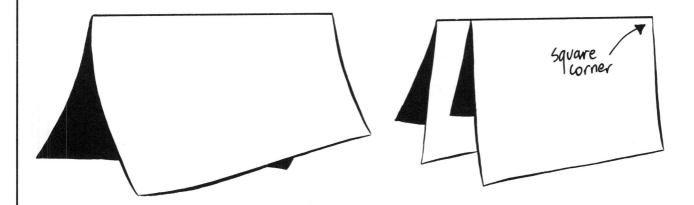

square corner

3 Use it to test for right angles, for example corners of books, corners of tables, etc.

USING A PROTRACTOR

1 Use a protractor to measure these angles:

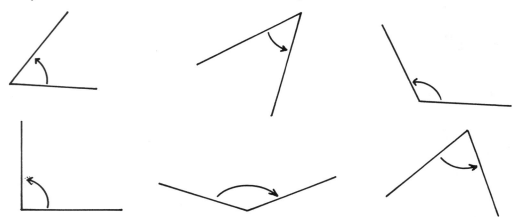

2 Estimate and then measure the sizes of these angles:

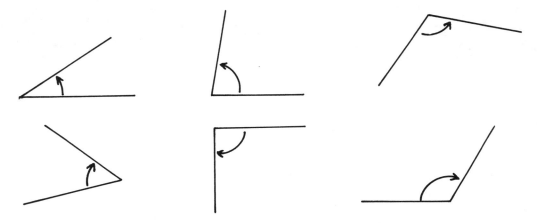

3 How could you use your protractor to help you copy this angle?

4 Use a protractor to draw angles of:

50°   80°   66°   90°   12°

FINDING RIGHT ANGLES

1 How many right angles can you find in each of these:
  a the blackboard
  b a window
  c a chalk box
  d a classroom cupboard?

2 Find at least three other different examples of right angles.

3 Why are right angles so common?

ANGLE PARKING

1 Find an angle-parking sign. At what angle should the vehicles be parked?

2 Make a large cardboard model of this angle and use it to determine which vehicles are correctly parked.

WHAT ANGLE IS IT?

Through what angle:
a can you turn your head
b can you bend your elbow
c do you turn a key to open a door
d do you unscrew a lid to remove it from a jar?

FINDING THE ANGLE SUM OF A TRIANGLE

1 Draw a triangle (of any shape) on a piece of paper and cut it out. Mark its angles; then tear them off and place them together like this

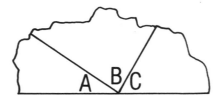

What have you discovered?

2 Using a protractor, find the sizes of the following angles:

a
A =
B =
C =
Sum of angles =

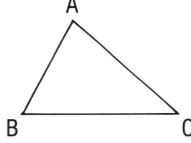

b
P =
Q =
R =
Sum of angles =

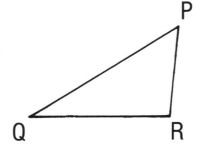

c Repeat, using a triangle of any shape.

d What have you discovered?

CREATIVE DESIGNS

1 Draw a circle and mark off the radius six times around its circumference. Join every second mark to obtain an equilateral triangle. Find the midpoint of each side and join to the opposite vertex. Then draw triangles as shown. What shape are they? Then shade as shown.

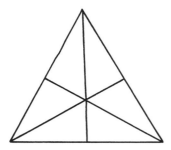 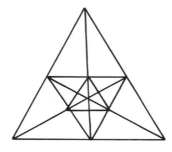 

2 Now make a triangular design of your own.

3 Draw a circle and use a protractor to mark off five equally spaced points around the circumference. (What angle will you need to turn through each time?) Use these five points to obtain the following design:

4 Draw another circle and mark off five equally spaced points around it. Now join the points in any way to create your own construction.

5 Make a design using ten equally spaced points around a circle.

DRAWING SPIRALS

1 Draw a two-center spiral as follows:

a Draw a line across your page and mark two points A and B fairly close together on it.

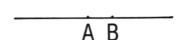

b With center A and radius AB draw a half-circle.

c Then with center B and radius BC draw a further half-circle starting from the end-point of the previous one.

d Then using center A and starting from the endpoint of the second half-circle, continue the process.

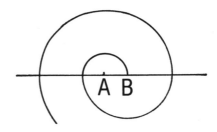

2 A four-center spiral may be formed in a similar way by drawing quarter circles, using as centers the vertices of a square A, B, C, D, A, . . . in succession. Try it.

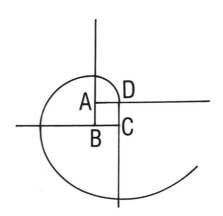

A SPIRALING SPOOL

Obtain a spiral by following these steps:

1 Wind a length of string onto a spool and make a loop for a pencil in the free end of the string.

2 Secure the spool (so that it cannot move) on the center of a piece of paper.

3 Place a pencil in the string's loop and begin to draw in a circular motion around the spool. (A spiral will form as the string unwinds.)

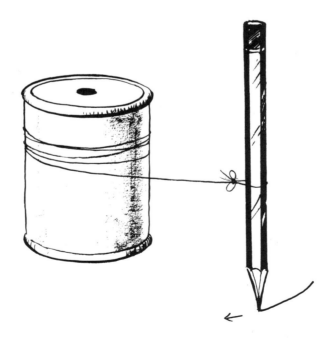

INVESTIGATING SQUARES AND RECTANGLES

1 Copy this square and its diagonals into your book:

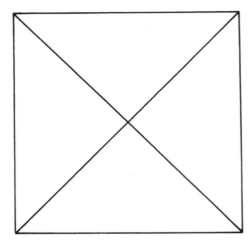

2 Using a protractor, measure sizes of various angles and with a ruler find lengths of various sides and intervals. What have you discovered?

3 Repeat similar investigations for this rectangle and its diagonals:

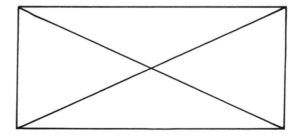

4 Compare the results for both the square and the rectangle. How are they similar? How do they differ?

INVESTIGATING PARALLELOGRAMS AND RHOMBUSES

1 Measure sizes of angles and lengths of intervals for this parallelogram and its diagonals:

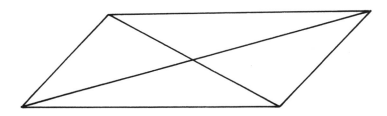

2 Record your results.

3 Conduct similar investigations for this rhombus and its diagonals:

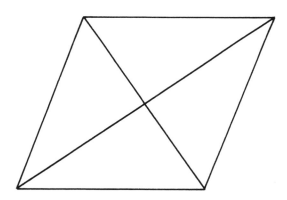

4 Record your results.

5 Compare results for each. How are they similar? How do they differ?

FINDING TRIANGLES AND SQUARES

1 Ring those words below that name the corners of a triangle in the letter pattern at the right:

TEN   DAM
PEN   DIN
BOX   MOB
DIG   DOG

```
B   U   S   X

G   T   I   D

C   E   O   A

H   N   P   M
```

List other words that name the corners of a triangle.

2 Ring those words that name the corners of a square:

FISH   PEAL
CART   SHIP
DEAR   BEAM
HOME   THEM

```
T   F   H   C

O   I   S   G

P   B   D   E

L   M   R   A
```

List words that name the corners of a rectangle.

MARKING OUT A PLAYING FIELD

Follow these steps to mark out a rectangular playing field (10 meters by 6 meters):

1 Place a peg in the ground at A and then measure 10 meters to B.

2 Turn through an estimated right angle and measure 6 meters to C.

3 Turn through another right angle and measure 10 meters to D.

4 Move D, if necessary, so that its distance from A is 6 meters.

5 Then the shape of ABCD must be at least a parallelogram. Why? To determine if it is a rectangle measure AC and BD. Why?

6 If necessary move C and D until AC equals BD (making sure that CD remains 10 meters in length while each of AD and BC remains 6 meters in length).

TRIANGLES AND HEXAGONS

Photocopy (or trace) these shapes and cut them out:

1   Use the six equilateral triangles to form another hexagon like A.

2   Using the hexagon (A) and the six triangles, form a six-pointed star.

3   Using the hexagon (A) and some of the triangles make:
   a a large triangle
   b a shape with one axis of symmetry
   c a shape with two axes of symmetry.
   (Try to find two different solutions for each of **b** and **c**.)

4   Various shapes may be formed using two or more triangles if they are placed so that a side of one touches an entire side of another like this:

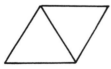

not like this:

What shape(s) can be formed using:
a two triangles
b three triangles
c four triangles?

DISCOVERING TETROMINOES AND PENTOMINOES

1 Obtain some square grid paper. Color in four squares that are joined together along their edges, for example:

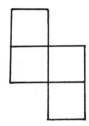

2 Show that the shape above can be moved (by flipping and/or turning) to the shape shown below (which is not therefore a different shape):

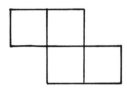

3 How many different shapes can you form by coloring four squares? (These are called tetrominoes. You should be able to find five of them.)

4 Now color in five squares so that they join along edges. How many different shapes can you form? (These are called pentominoes. You should be able to find 12 of them.)

ACTIVITIES WITH TETROMINOES

1 Using cardboard (or thin styrene) make a set of tetrominoes:

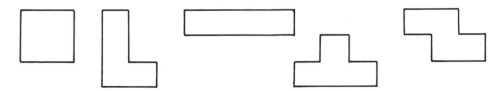

2 Draw each of the five tetromino shapes and mark in any lines of symmetry for each.

3 Can you form tessellations using, in turn, each of the tetromino pieces?

4 Make a square base equal in area to 25 square tiles from which you made your set of tetrominoes. Shade in five squares as shown. Now see if you can cover the remainder of the square using the five tetromino pieces.

Can you make up another puzzle like this one?

ACTIVITIES WITH PENTOMINOES

1 Obtain (or make) a set of pentominoes.

2 Which pieces are symmetrical?

3 Which pieces tessellate?

4 Can you form a 6 by 5 rectangle using six of the 12 pieces?

5 Can you form a rectangle (10 units long and 6 units wide) using your set of pentominoes?

6 Can you form a 12 by 5 rectangle — or a 15 by 4 rectangle?

SHAPES ON A GEOBOARD

For these activities you will need at least a 5 by 5 geoboard (pinboard).

1 Form a square of side 1 unit on the geoboard. What is its area?

2 Form as many different shapes as you can with an area of 2 square units. Can you form a square with this area?

3 Form shapes having an area of 3 square units.

4 Form shapes having an area of 4 square units.

5 How many different shapes with a perimeter of 12 units can you form?

```
.   .   .   .   .

.   .   .   .   .

.   .   .   .   .

.   .   .   .   .

.   .   .   .   .
```

TESSELLATIONS

Draw six more of each of the shapes below so that they tessellate (that is, so that there are no gaps or overlaps):

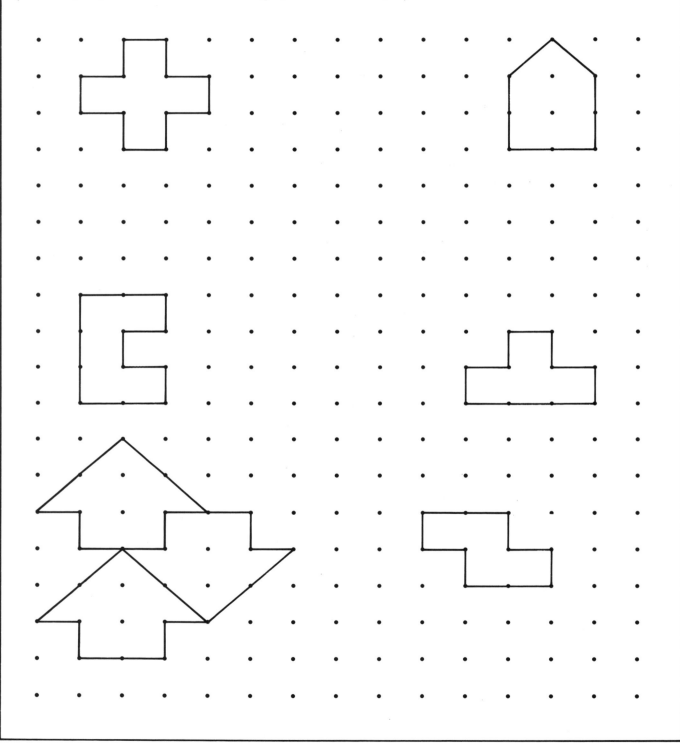

WHICH ONES?

These are GEODS:

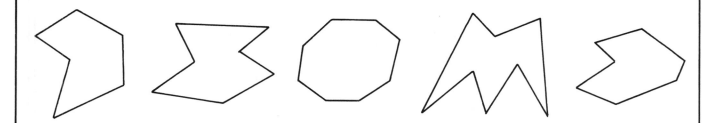

These are not GEODS:

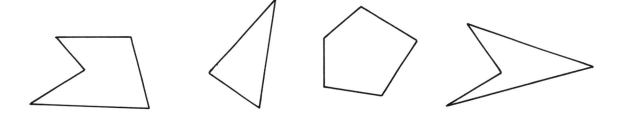

Which of these are GEODS?

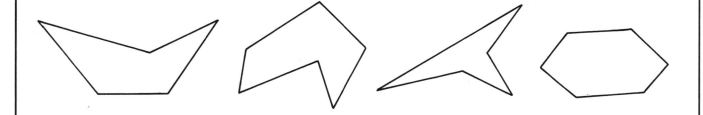

FINDING CIRCUMFERENCES AND DIAMETERS

1 **a** Select a circle (circular face of a cylinder) and trace around it onto a piece of paper. Cut out the circle and fold it in half. How can you now find the length of the diameter?

    b Find the circumference of the same circle by wrapping a piece of string around the cylinder.

    c Record both results in the table below.

2 Repeat the procedure for a differently sized circle.

3 **a** Select a third circle. Can you find its diameter by placing it between two set squares held upright on the desk like this?

    b Can you find the circumference of the circle by rolling it along the desk?

    c Record results in the table:

	Diameter	Circumference
1		
2		
3		

4 How does the circumference compare with the diameter in each case? (A calculator may be useful.)

5 Test out your guess with another circle.

6 *Application:* What is the circumference of a bicycle wheel with a diameter of 70 cm? How many times would the wheel turn to travel 1 kilometer? How could you use this bicycle to mark out a distance of 100 meters?

SHADOWS FROM SOLIDS

1 Put a large sheet of white paper on a table. Place the table near a window (or in front of a desk lamp) so that you can form shadows. On the sheet of paper place the following solids and draw the shadow of each of them:

 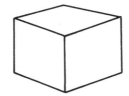 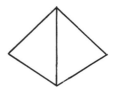

a a cylinder   **b** a cube   **c** a square pyramid.

2 Now try shadows for these:
 a a sphere
 b a triangular prism
 c a cone.

3 Find solids that could produce shadows like these:

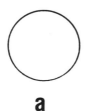

a   **b**   **c**   **d**   **e**

4 Which of these could not be shadows of a cone:

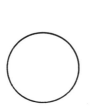   

SLICING THROUGH SOLIDS

1   Using clay or plasticene make models of these:
    a a cylinder
    b a cone
    c a cube
    d a square pyramid.

2   Cut through the cylinder at right angles to its axis and describe the shape of the cut:

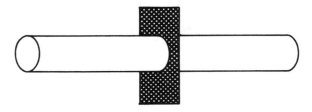

3   Cut through the cylinder obliquely like this; what shape is the cut?

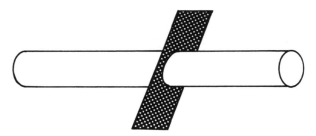

4   Cut through the cylinder like this; what shape is the cut?

5   Cut through the other solids in differing ways and describe your results.

POINT OF VIEW

1 Each side of a structure with a square base is like this:

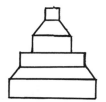

Which of these is the top view?

A  B  C  D

2 Each side view of a structure with a square base is:

Draw the top view.

3 The top view of a structure is:

Which of these could be a side view?

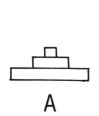 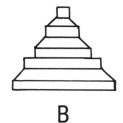 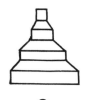   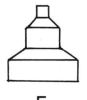

A   B   C   D   E

FACES, VERTICES, AND EDGES

1 Count the number of vertices, faces, and edges for each of these solids and record your results in the table:

a Cube

b Square pyramid

c Triangular prism

d Tetrahedron

e Hexagonal prism

Vertices	Faces	Edges

2 Can you see a pattern?

3 Does it hold for a hexagonal pyramid?

PUZZLES WITH SOLID SHAPES

1 The sketch shows a cube with one vertex removed. If all the vertices are removed in the same way, the new solid will have how many:
a faces
b edges
c vertices?

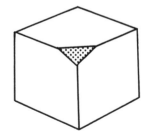

2 This cube is made of wire. If an ant starts at A, what is the greatest number of edges that it can walk along if it must not leave the wire nor travel along the same edge twice?

3 **a** What is the least number of edges the ant must walk along when going from A to B?
b What is the greatest number of edges the ant can walk along when going from A to B (if the ant must not travel any edge more than once)?

4 Which of these cannot be nets for a cube?

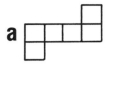 **a**

 b

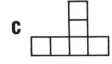 **c**

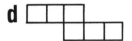 **d**

 **e**

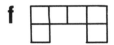 **f**

 g

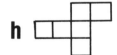 **h**

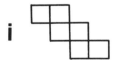 **i**

DRAWING CUBES

1 On the grid draw cubes with sides of 2, 3, and 4 units. (The 1 unit cube has been drawn.) Each starting point is shown.

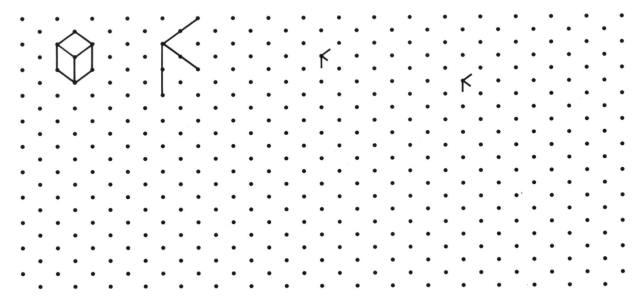

2 On the grid below each shape, draw how it will look if a cube is added to each shaded face:

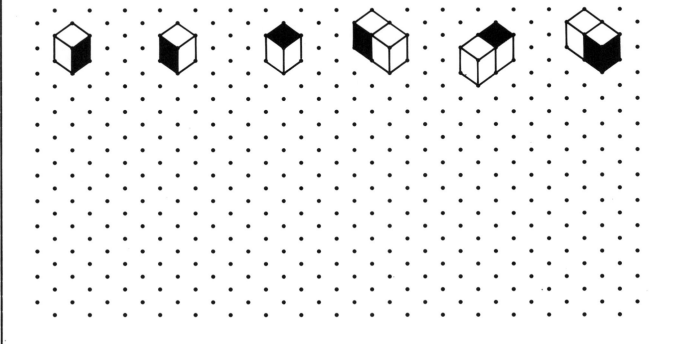

THE PLATONIC SOLIDS

If available, use Polydron pieces to make the five regular solids (platonic solids) shown below:

a Tetrahedron

b Cube

c Octahedron

d Dodecahedron

e Icosahedron

or make them from light cardboard by tracing and cutting out these nets:

 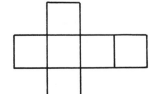 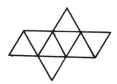

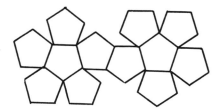 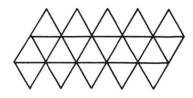

For each, record the number of faces, vertices and edges.

SOMA CUBES

1   Obtain (or make) a set of pieces that form a Soma cube:

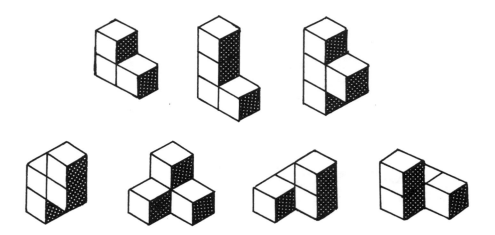

2   Select the first three pieces (above) and see how many different shapes you can make from these three pieces.

3   Place all seven pieces together to form a cube.

4   Use the seven pieces to make these shapes:

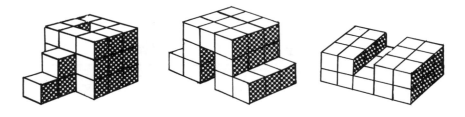

The well   The tunnel   The canal

CUTTING A CIRCLE

1 What approach would you use to solve this problem:

   ● What is the greatest number of parts into which a circle may be cut by ten straight lines?

2 Make a guess of the answer.

3 a Complete this table:

Number of cuts	Number of parts
0	1
1	
2	
3	
4	

   b Can you see a pattern?

4 How many parts are there for:
   a five cuts?
   b ten cuts?

SQUARES ON A GEOBOARD

Consider this problem:

- How many squares are there on an 8 by 8 geoboard (or on a chessboard)?

1 Find five squares in this figure:

2 Can you find 14 squares in this figure?

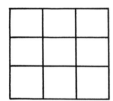

3 Now try a 4 by 4 square.

4 Now try the 8 by 8 square as follows:

- number of 1 by 1 squares =
- number of 2 by 2 squares =
- number of 3 by 3 squares =
- number of 4 by 4 squares =
- number of 5 by 5 squares =
- number of 6 by 6 squares =
- number of 7 by 7 squares =
- number of 8 by 8 squares =
- total number of squares   =

A PATTERN WITH DIAGONALS

Can you guess the number of diagonals in a decagon (ten-sided figure)? (Diagonals join vertices.)

To determine the answer we will consider some simpler cases and search for a pattern to help us.

1 Find the diagonals in the following figures by drawing the diagonals and counting them. Record your answers in the table:

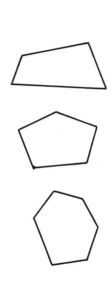

Number of sides	Number of diagonals
4	
5	
6	
7	14

(The answer for a seven-sided polygon is given to help you.)

2 See if you can extend the pattern to eight, nine, ten . . . sides. Try to find at least two different ways of obtaining this pattern.

HOW MANY RECTANGLES?

1 In Figure A there are some differently sized and differently shaped rectangles. How many are like each of the rectangles drawn below?

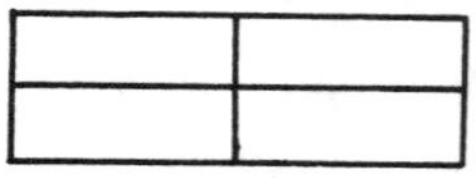

A

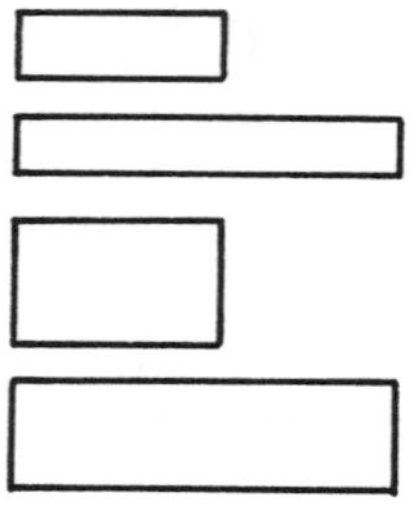

2 Find the total number of rectangles in Figure B by first counting the number of rectangles like each of those drawn below and then adding them all together to give you the total.

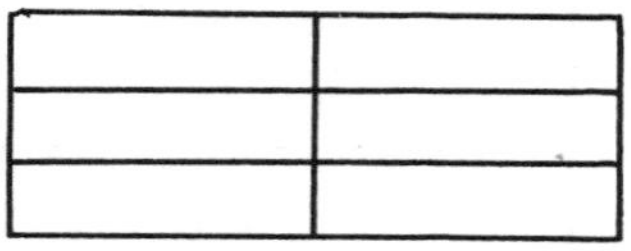

B

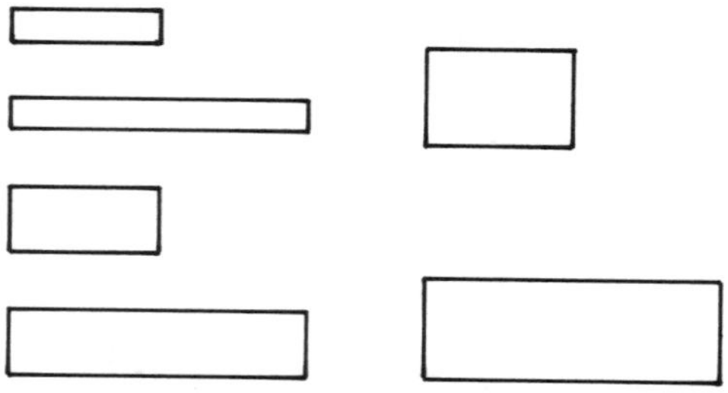

3 Find the total number of rectangles in Figure C.

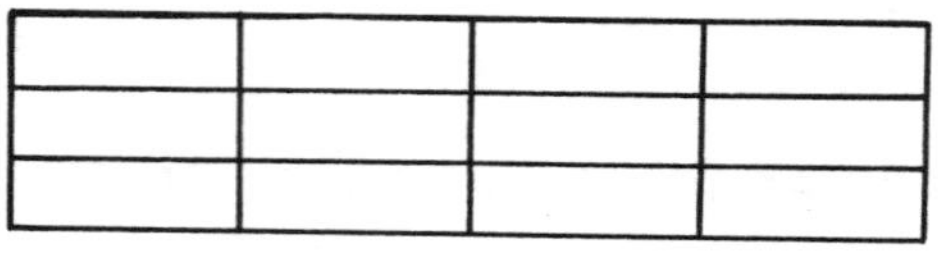

C

HOW MANY TRIANGLES?

1 There are eight different triangles in this figure. One of them is made up of regions 1 and 4. List the other seven of them.

2 How many triangles are in each of these?

a

b

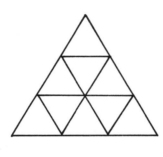
c

3 Find the total number of triangles in each of these figures:

a

b

c

d

INSIDE OR OUTSIDE?

1 In each of the following, B is outside the closed curve while A is either inside or outside it. State whether A is inside or outside and record the number of times that the interval AB crosses the boundary:

A (inside or outside?)   Number of crossings

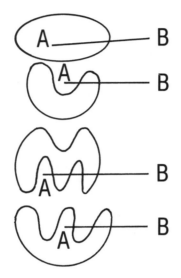

2 Can you see a rule? If so, complete this:

● To determine whether a point is inside or outside a closed curve, join the point to a point that is outside. Then count the number of times that this interval crosses the curve. For an .... number of crossings it is outside, while for an .... number of crossings it is inside.

3 Now use this rule to find whether the cross is inside or outside:

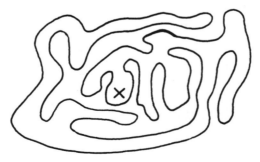

4 Make up some puzzles of your own.

KONIGSBERG BRIDGE PROBLEM

Two islands are joined to each other and to each side of the river by means of seven bridges. Is it possible to cross each bridge once and once only?

A network consists of points (vertices) connected by arcs (straight or curved), for example

A vertex (point) is *even* if an even number of arcs meet at it while it is *odd* if an odd number of arcs meet at it. A network is *traversable* (traceable) if it can be drawn without lifting pencil from paper and without redrawing any line. It is *unicursal* if we can end the drawing at the starting point.

1 For each network below, count the number of even vertices and the number of odd vertices. Determine if the network is traversable and if it is unicursal:

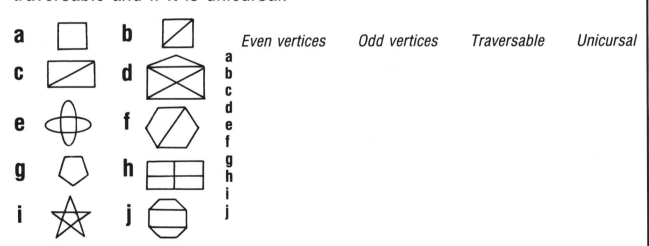

		Even vertices	Odd vertices	Traversable	Unicursal
a					
b					
c					
d					
e					
f					
g					
h					
i					
j					

2 Can you discover a pattern? If so complete these:
- A network is traversable only if
- A network is unicursal only if

3 The Konigsberg bridges can be represented by this network: Is it traversable?

MAZES

A maze may be constructed as follows:

1 Draw a square-like shape open at upper left and lower right:

2 Add interior lines (straight or curved) so that each new line only meets one previously drawn line, for example:

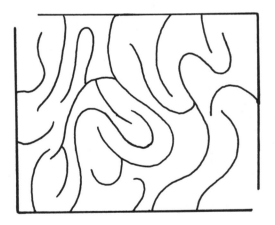

3 Now solve your maze.

4 Construct another maze and ask your neighbor to solve it.

EXPERIMENTS WITH A MOBIUS STRIP

1 Make a Mobius strip by first cutting out a rectangular strip of paper about 30 cm long and 3 cm wide, then giving the strip a half twist and taping the ends together.

2 Cut the Mobius strip along a line midway between each edge. What happens? Cut this new strip in half, too. What now happens?

3 Make another Mobius strip and cut along a line one-third the distance from one edge. What results?

4 Carry out your own experiments. (For example, take a rectangular piece of paper and give it two twists before taping the ends together. Cut it in half, etc.)

DRAWING AXES OF SYMMETRY

1 Use geostrips to make these triangles, having zero, one and three axes of symmetry:

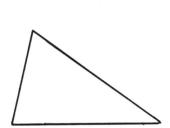 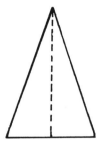 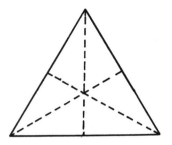

2 Use geostrips to make (where possible) a quadrilateral having:

  a zero axes of symmetry

  b one axis of symmetry

  c two axes of symmetry

  d three axes of symmetry

  e four axes of symmetry.

3 Can you make pentagons with only one axis of symmetry? Can you make a pentagon with exactly two axes of symmetry? Test for three, four, or five axes of symmetry.

4 Repeat the same for hexagons.

5 Can you see a rule emerging? Test it for an octagon.

6 What are the possibilities for a dodecagon (12-sided polygon)?

SYMMETRY OF REGULAR POLYGONS

A polygon is any plane shape with three or more sides. It is regular if all of its sides are equal and all of its angles are equal.

1 Estimate the number of axes of symmetry that a regular 90-sided figure has.

2 To determine this number follow these steps:

a How many axes of symmetry are there in each of these shapes? (You may either use a mirror on these or fold cutouts of them.)

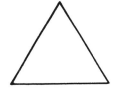 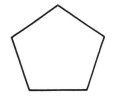  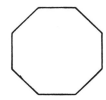

b Now predict the number of axes of symmetry in a regular 90-sided figure; in a regular 99-sided figure.

3 Did you notice that in the equilateral triangle each line of symmetry joins a vertex to the midpoint of the opposite side? For what other figure(s) is this the case? What points were joined in the square?

4 Where would the lines be for a regular 90-sided figure? Where for a regular 99-sided figure?

SIZES OF ANGLES OF REGULAR POLYGONS

1 a Draw a square on the floor (or find a square piece of concrete). Start at one corner and walk along each boundary back to your starting point (and face in the same direction as you did to begin).

b Through what angle did you turn at each corner? (Notice that these angles are the ones dotted on the diagram.)

c Through how many degrees did you turn in your total movement (from start to finish)?

2 a Trace a pencil along the boundary of this equilateral triangle.

b Through how many degrees do you turn from start to finish?

c Through what exterior angle (indicated by dots) do you turn at each corner?

d What is the size of each interior angle (shown by a cross) of the equilateral triangle?

3 a Through how many degrees do you turn from start to finish?

b Through what exterior angle do you turn at each corner?

c Therefore what is the size of each interior angle?

4 In the same way find the size of each interior angle of a regular hexagon.

WHICH REGULAR POLYGONS TESSELLATE?

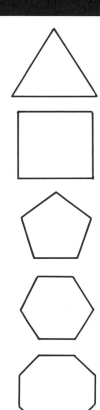

1 Trace these regular polygons onto a piece of paper and cut out at least six of each shape:

2 Do equilateral triangles tessellate, that is, can they be placed without gaps or without overlapping?

3 Repeat, in turn, for squares, pentagons, regular hexagons, and regular octagons. Which of these regular shapes tessellate?

4 Can you find examples of these tessellations in the environment?

5 You should have noticed that only three of the above shapes tessellate. In fact, no other regular polygons will tessellate. We will now discover why this is so:

  a Using the results of the previous activity, "Sizes of Angles of Regular Polygons," complete this table:

Regular polygon	Size of each interior angle
Equilateral triangle	
Square	
Regular pentagon	
Regular hexagon	

  b If a regular polygon tessellates, each of its interior angles must be a factor of 360 degrees. Why?

  c Therefore, which regular shapes only will tessellate?

Challenging Extension Activities

MAKING A CLINOMETER

1 Draw (or trace) the following shape onto a piece of pasteboard:

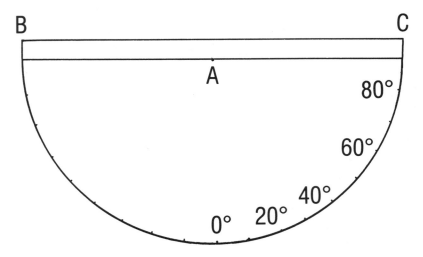

2 Make a hole at A and through it attach a weighted string. Along BC tape a straw (through which to sight).

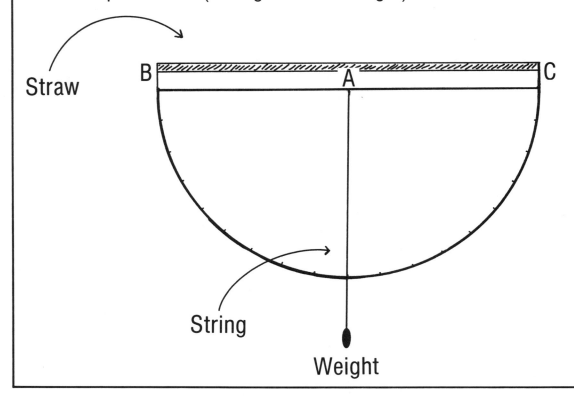

USING A CLINOMETER

Use your clinometer to find the height of a flagpole as follows:

1 First estimate the height of the flagpole.

2 Stand at a convenient distance from the flagpole on ground level with its base and use your clinometer to find the angle to the top of the flagpole.

3 Measure the distance from where you are standing to the flagpole. Also measure the height of your eye level.

4 Make a scale drawing using the measurements so obtained:

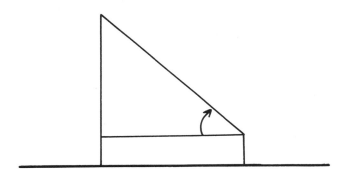

5 Avoid the need for a scale drawing by choosing the place where you stand so that the angle is 45 degrees. The height of the flagpole will be your distance from the flagpole plus the height of your eye level. Why?

HEIGHTS WITH A SET SQUARE

1   Select an object whose height you want to find (e.g. a pine tree, a flagpole).

2   Place a table on ground that is level with the base of the object.

3   Hold vertically a 45-degree set square on the table and sight along its hypotenuse (side opposite the right angle). Slide it along the table (and move the table if necessary) until you can sight the top of the object.

4   Measure along the ground from the set square to the object.

5   Then the height of the object will be that distance plus the height of the table.

6   Can you explain why?

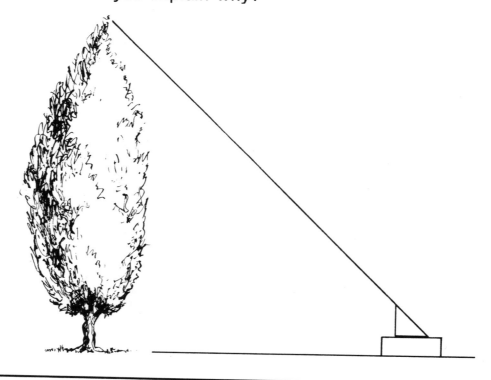

THREE TOPS IN A LINE

1 Estimate the height of a flagpole (or some suitable object).

2 Now find its height as follows:

a find a partner whose height is the same as yours;

b lie on ground that is level with the base of the flagpole so that your feet are facing the flagpole while your partner stands at your feet;

c move until you can sight the top of the flagpole in line with the top of your partner's head (your partner moves, too, so that he is always standing upright at your feet);

d use a trundle wheel to measure the distance from the flagpole to where your head was on the ground — this is equal to the height of the flagpole.

3 Can you explain why the method works? (Variation: You could use a tomato stake cut to your height instead of a partner but you will need someone to hold it upright at your feet.)

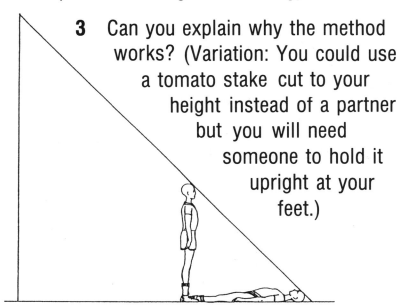

DISTANCE ACROSS A ROADWAY

1 Select a roadway (or creek or pond). Estimate the distance across it.

2 Now determine that distance as follows:

   a Observe some prominent feature (e.g. a post, tree, etc. marked A) close to the edge on the side opposite to where you are standing at B.

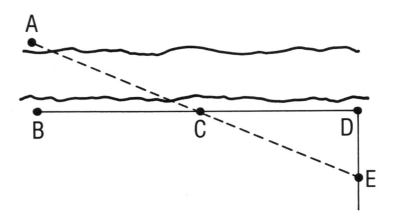

   b Measure from B to C (by pacing or using a trundle wheel). If needed, place a stick upright in the ground at C.

   c Continue in the same direction from C to D so that the distance CD is the same as BC.

   d At D turn through a right angle and continue until A and C are in line at E.

   e Measure DE. This will be equal to AB. Why?

FINDING THE WIDTH OF A POOL

Discovery: In each of these triangles the midpoints of two sides of the triangle have been joined:

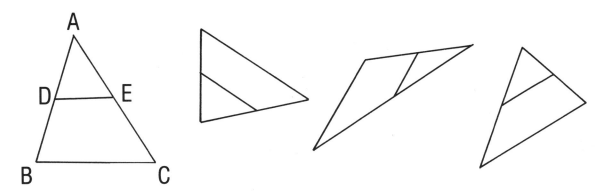

By observation can you guess how the length of DE compares with the length of BC? Check by measurement. Repeat for the other three triangles. What have you found?

Application: To find the width AB of a small pool or dam.

1   Select a convenient point C and measure (by pacing or with a trundle wheel) the distance from A to C:

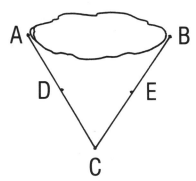

2   Then find D, the midpoint of AC, by measuring halfway back from C to A.

3   Measure BC and locate E its midpoint.

4   Measure from D to E. This will be half the width of the pool. Why?

BISECTING ANGLES

1 Copy this angle onto your page:

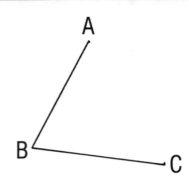

2 Now bisect it as follows: With center B and a convenient radius, draw arcs to cut AB at D and BC at E. With center D and a suitable radius draw an arc. With center E and the same radius draw a second arc to cut the other at F. Join BF; it will bisect angle ABC.

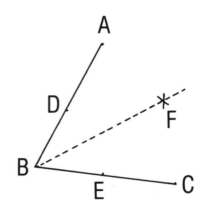

3 Copy and bisect this angle:

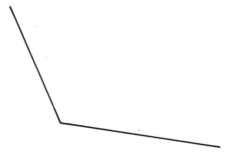

4 Can you find examples of angle bisection? Is a mitered joint an example?

DRAWING A REGULAR OCTAGON

1 Draw a circle, center O, and draw a diameter AB.

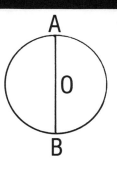

2 Construct a perpendicular diameter CD. You can do this as follows:
(With A as center and a suitable radius draw an arc; with B as center and the same radius draw a second arc to cut the first at P. Use PO to obtain CD.)

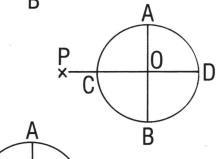

3 Bisect angle AOC and obtain E on the circumference.

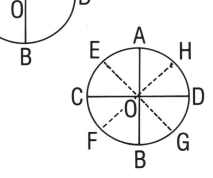

4 Either extend EO to G and obtain F and H by bisecting angle COB, or step off AE around the circumference.

5 Join A, E, C . . ., H, A.

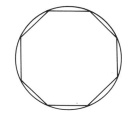

6 Create a design based on the regular octagon, for example:

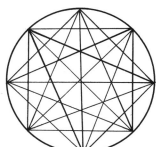

(You could shade alternate regions.)

CONSTRUCTING TRIANGLES

1 Follow the steps below to construct a triangle ABC so that BC is 10 cm, AB is 8 cm and AC is 7 cm:

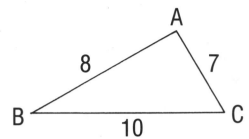

a Draw an interval BC of length 10 cm:

b With center B and a radius of 8 cm draw an arc above BC; with center C and the same radius draw a second arc to cut the first arc at A:

B ———————————— C

c Join AB and AC.

2 Construct a triangle with sides of length 9 cm, 7 cm, 5 cm.

3 Construct a triangle with sides of length 8 cm, 8 cm, 5 cm. What is special about it?

4 Is it possible to construct a triangle with sides 8 cm, 4 cm, 3 cm? Why?

THE 3, 4, 5 TRIANGLE

1 Construct triangles with sides of:
a 3 cm, 4 cm, 5 cm
b 6 cm, 8 cm, 10 cm
c 7.5 cm, 10 cm, 12.5 cm
d 9 cm, 12 cm, 15 cm.

2 What is special about each of these triangles?

3 a Cut a piece of string 120 cm long. Put a mark on it 30 cm from one end and a mark 50 cm from the other end:

30 cm   40 cm   50 cm

b Use this piece of string to form a triangle by joining the two ends for one vertex (corner) and having the marks at the other two vertices. What kind of a triangle is it?

4 Where (and in what situations) are these special triangles of practical use?

INVESTIGATING TRIANGLES (1)

1 Copy this triangle onto a piece of paper and cut it out:

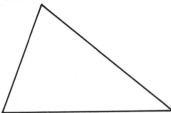

2 Find the midpoint of each side. Join each of these to the opposite vertex. (These lines are called medians:) What do you notice about how the medians cross?

3 We say that these three medians are concurrent (i.e. they pass through the same point). How far along each median is this point?

4 Try balancing your triangle at this point. (This point is the center of gravity of the triangle.)

5 **a** Copy the following figure:

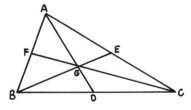

  b Join F and E, E and D, and F and D. What do you notice about the triangle that you have formed?

  c Can you discover some special quadrilaterals (e.g. parallelograms)?

  d Are there any intervals of equal length?

INVESTIGATING TRIANGLES (2)

1 Copy this triangle onto a piece of paper and cut it out:

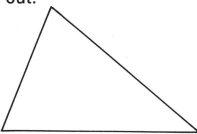

2 Find the perpendicular bisector of a side by folding as shown (making two vertices coincide).

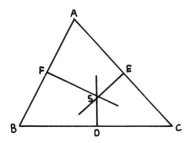

3 Open the paper back out and fold the perpendicular bisectors of each of the other two sides in turn. What do you notice about how they meet?

4 Did you obtain a result like this?

5 Measure the distance of S from each of A, B, and C. What did you find? Can you now explain how to draw a circle through A, B, and C?

6 Test your theory on a different triangle.

NOTES FOR TEACHERS

(including some solutions)

Shape walk (p. 3)
Which shapes occur more frequently?
Why?

Symmetrical figures and lines of symmetry (pp. 4, 5)
Some prior experiences include:
a forming symmetrical shapes with assorted shapes such as pattern blocks;
b forming symmetrical shapes on a geoboard;
c making symmetrical collages using environmental materials such as leaves, seeds and/or grass;
d having a symmetry hunt (locating symmetrical objects in the environment).

Pupils may think of the line of symmetry as a balance line; so that one half of the shape would flip over and match the other half.

A five-piece tangram (p. 11)
A five-piece tangram simply consists of five pieces. Another way of obtaining five pieces would be to cut a square as follows:

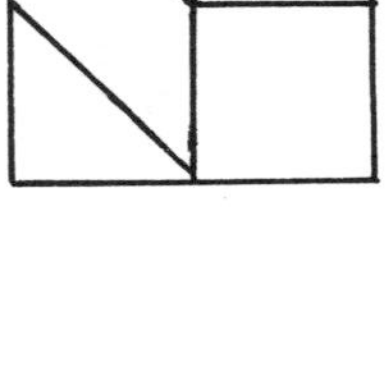

Exploring with tangrams (p. 13)
1 Triangles can also be formed from three pieces using:
   a the two small triangles and the middle-sized triangle
   b the two small triangles and the parallelogram.
6 In turn, cover each shape with the two small triangles.

Rigid shapes (p. 16)
Pupils could compile a table showing the number of sides of the shape and the number of diagonal braces required to make it rigid:

- Number of sides of shape   4 5 6 7 8
- Number of diagonal braces   1 2 3

They will find that the number of diagonal braces required is 3 less than the number of sides.

Forming triangles (p. 16)
The basic concept underlying this activity is:
- In any triangle the sum of any two sides is always greater than the third side.

Hence a triangle with sides 4 cm, 5 cm and 10 cm does not exist.

Shapes on a geoboard
(p. 47)

5 There are many different shapes with a perimeter of 12 units, for example:

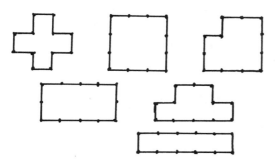

Which ones? (p. 49)
The second and fourth are GEODS (which have six or more sides).

Faces, vertices, and edges
(p. 54)
The sum of the number of faces and the number of vertices is 2 more than the number of edges.

Puzzles with solid shapes (p. 55)
1 **a** Number of faces $= 6 + 8 = 14$
   b Number of edges
      $= 12 + 8 \times 3 = 36$
   c Number of vertices $= 8 \times 3$
      $= 24$
2 Nine edges.
3 **a** Three edges.
   b Seven edges.

A pattern with diagonals
(p. 61)
The table is:

4	2
5	5
6	9
7	14
8	20
9	27

- Notice that $2 + 3 = 5$; $5 + 4 = 9$; $9 + 5 = 14$; $14 + 6 = 20$; and so on.
- Also notice that $4 \times \frac{1}{2} = 2$; $5 \times 1 = 5$; $6 \times 1\frac{1}{2} = 9$; $7 \times 2 = 14$; and so on.
- Also notice that for a six-sided polygon, $3 + 3 + 2 + 1 = 9$; for an eight-sided polygon $5 + 5 + 4 + 3 + 2 + 1 = 20$ etc., so that for a 15-sided polygon the number of diagonals would be $12 + 12 + 11 + 10 + \ldots + 3 + 2 + 1 = 90$.

Konigsberg bridge problem
(p. 65)
2 A network is traversable only if there are no more than two odd vertices. A network is unicursal only if there are no odd vertices.

Drawing axes of symmetry
(p. 68)
It is possible to draw quadrilaterals having 0, 1, 2, and 4 axes of symmetry, pentagons, with 0, 1, and 5 axes of symmetry, and hexagons with 0, 1, 2, 3, and 6 axes of symmetry. The number of axes is a factor of the number of sides (besides the case of zero factors). Dodecagons exist with 0, 1, 2, 3, 4, 6, and 12 axes of symmetry.

Symmetry of regular polygons (p. 69)

For regular polygons we have:

Number of sides	Number of axes of symmetry
3	3
4	4
5	5
6	6

Thus a regular 90-sided figure would have 90 axes of symmetry. In the case of regular polygons with an odd number of sides, the axes of symmetry join each vertex to the midpoint of the opposite side. For regular polygons with an even number of sides half the axes of symmetry join opposite vertices while the other half join midpoints of opposite sides.

Sizes of angles of regular polygons (p. 70)

This exploration correlates well with Apple Logo work involving the movement of the turtle.

To draw any polygon, a total turn of 360 degrees (from start to finish) is involved (if one ends facing the same way as at the start). Thus to find the size of each exterior angle, simply divide 360 degrees by the number of sides. The interior angle is then found by subtracting this amount from 180 degrees.

Which regular polygons tessellate? (p. 71)

Only three regular polygons tessellate: the equilateral triangle, the square and the regular hexagon. Each angle of an equilateral triangle is 60 degrees so that six of them fit together at a point. Four squares meet at a point since each angle is 90 degrees. Three regular hexagons meet at a point since each angle is 120 degrees.

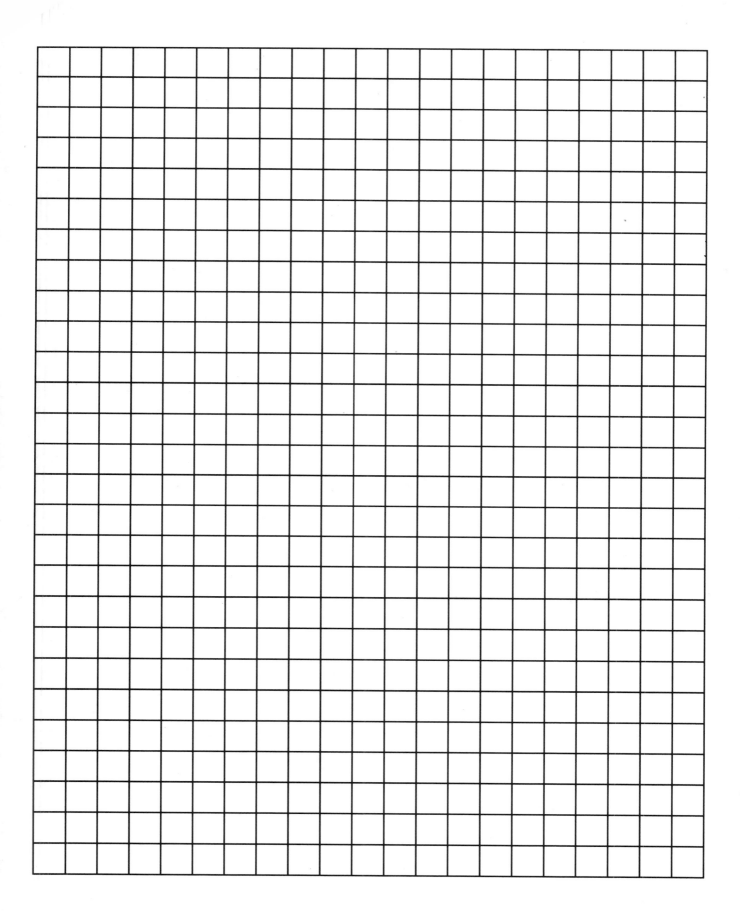